S0-BEA-825

Ronald A. Nykiel, PhD
Elizabeth Jascolt, MHM

Marketing Your City, U.S.A.
A Guide to Developing a Strategic Tourism Marketing Plan

More pre-publication
REVIEWS, COMMENTARIES, EVALUATIONS . . .

"**A**n interesting marketing 'how to' book for a city desirous of increasing their share of the explosion in revenue available from tourism. Also an excellent guide for a city interested in maximizing the effectiveness of an existing tourism marketing plan. The book provides solutions to tourism marketing problems at the grassroots level."

Alan T. Stutts, PhD, CHE
Dean and Barron Hilton Distinguished Chair, Conrad N. Hilton College of Hotel and Restaurant Management, University of Houston

"**M**arketing Your City will certainly be an excellent guide for anyone involved in the planning and marketing of cities and regions. Nykiel and Jascolt did a terrific job of synthesizing an otherwise complex procedure."

James C. Maken, PhD
Associate Professor, Babcock Graduate School of Management, Wake Forest University, Winston-Salem, NC

The Haworth Hospitality Press
An Imprint of The Haworth Press
New York • London

Marketing Your City, U.S.A.
A Guide to Developing a Strategic Tourism Marketing Plan

Marketing Your City, U.S.A.
A Guide to Developing a Strategic Tourism Marketing Plan

Ronald A. Nykiel, PhD
Elizabeth Jascolt, MHM

The Haworth Hospitality Press
An Imprint of The Haworth Press
New York • London

Published by

The Haworth Hospitality Press, an imprint of The Haworth Press, Inc., 10 Alice Street, Binghamton, NY 13904-1580

Cover design by Marylouise E. Doyle.

Library of Congress Cataloging-in-Publication Data

Nykiel, Ronald A.
  Marketing your city, U.S.A. : a guide to developing a strategic tourism marketing plan / Ronald A. Nykiel, Elizabeth Jascolt.
      p. cm.
  Includes bibliographical references and index.
  ISBN 0-7890-0591-3 (alk. paper).
  1. Tourist trade—United States. 2. Tourist trade—United States—Handbooks, manuals, etc.
I. Jascolt, Elizabeth. II. Title.
G155.U6N95 1998
338.4'7917304929—dc21   98-17980
                                                                                              CIP

CONTENTS

PART ONE:
THE STRATEGIC TOURISM MARKETING PLAN

PART TWO:
WORK FORMS

ABOUT THE AUTHORS

Ronald A. Nykiel, PhD, is the distinguished Chair and a Professor at the University of Houston's Conrad N. Hilton College of Hotel and Restaurant Management. He is a premiere international authority on hospitality and travel and tourism marketing, having served as a consultant to the President's Commissions, along with other federal and state entities and numerous corporations. He has appeared on national television and radio and has written various books and other publications about corporate strategy, marketing, consumer behavior, brand management, service excellence, and executive development topics. Dr. Nykiel is also the publisher of the *Hospitality Business Review.*

Elizabeth Jascolt, MHM, received her Bachelor of Commerce, Magna Cum Laude, with a major in marketing from the University of Ottawa in 1988. She began her business career with DuPont Canada, where she held positions in customer service, total quality management, and sales management for over seven years. Following this, she completed her Master of Hospitality Management at the University of Houston in 1997. She has worked as a restaurant manager at Walt Disney World in Orlando, Florida, and currently is Assistant Hotel Manager at Caesars Palace in Las Vegas, Nevada.

Preface

Cities, towns, and tourist areas enhance their services and infrastructures from the revenues generated by sales tax, room tax, and other taxes. Just as a corporation develops a strategic marketing plan to increase revenues, take market share, and promote new business, so too should cities, towns, and tourist areas. Revenue growth is the product of key marketing strategies that increase tourism, producing resultant increases in sales tax and room tax. These increased revenues allow for continued generation of growth in tourism through investment in infrastructure improvements and additional marketing programs.

This book provides those cities, towns, and tourist destinations seeking to enhance revenue growth through tourism with a step-by-step process to follow in preparing a strategic tourism marketing plan. Guidelines are provided for developing and selecting objectives, key strategies, and tactics to produce revenue and increased tourism. Specific examples of each step in the strategic tourism marketing planning process are provided using a theoretical destination—Your City, U.S.A.

In addition to the example step-by-step exhibits, specific marketing techniques and tools are delineated with actual examples. A sample promotional "calendar of events" provides a how-to example to plan and implement an ongoing series of promotions to fill every quarter and month of the year. An actual marketing plan budget is provided, showing how to allocate expenditures to each of the marketing categories: advertising, promotions, public relations, etc. Tactical steps and ideas are presented. Part Two has been designed to provide the reader with work forms that, when completed, result in the framework for a strategic tourism marketing plan.

Irrespective of the size of the city, town, or tourist destination, the strategic tourism marketing planning process will provide a plan format that, if successfully completed, will help enhance revenue growth and generate increased demand. It will further serve to prioritize ideas into objectives and strategies that will produce measurable results—increased revenues.

Ronald A. Nykiel, PhD
Elizabeth Jascolt, MHM

INTRODUCTION

MARKETING YOUR CITY, U.S.A.:
A GUIDE TO DEVELOPING
A STRATEGIC TOURISM MARKETING PLAN

A strategic tourism marketing plan is the basis for a win-win scenario for cities, towns, and tourist destinations as well as the businesses located within their boundaries. Cities, towns, and tourist areas enhance their services and infrastructure by the revenues generated from sales tax, room tax, and other taxes. As a greater number of retail sales and an increased number of room nights are generated, higher revenues and profit are produced from hospitality-based businesses within tourist communities. Just as a corporation views its strategic marketing plan as its road map to generating revenue, so too should cities, towns, and tourist destinations view their tourism marketing plans as their route to enhancing revenue. Frequently, this revenue is generated from taxes on visitors' expenditures within the tourist destination and so can be viewed as incremental revenue beyond that being paid by and collected from its residents. This is yet another win-win reason to have a strategic marketing plan for your community.

The hoteliers, restaurateurs, and retailers who collect these taxes from their customers (often having to justify their rates) have a right to and should participate in the development of their community's strategic tourism marketing plan. Selecting the right objectives and key strategies can result in increased business, stronger revenues, and greater profits. Likewise, the lack of such a plan or even selecting the wrong strategies can result in displaced revenue, lost business, and may even increase costs. In fact, the use of a strategic plan enables a community to make a better assessment of its future, thus making sound management decisions and putting itself in a position to influence its environment.[1]

Where should a city, town, or tourist destination begin with their strategic plans, and what structure should such a plan take? Utilizing a strategic marketing planning process, one not unlike that employed within a corporation, will help to formulate objectives, select strategies, identify required resources, target action steps, and, yes, produce measurable results. Similar to many corporate strategic plans, this process also includes ways to improve the "packaging" of your community to improve its visible appeal to tourists as well as to its local residents.

Let's briefly look at what such a plan is, what it should contain, and then at some concepts that will help organize your marketing ideas into productive action steps. Although the suggestions contained herein may not be applicable to every community or tourist destination, the strategic marketing planning process has universal application as a tool to assist your community in organizing objectives, developing strategies, and targeting revenue producing ideas.

Let's first start with describing what a strategic marketing plan is—a broad structure that guides the process of determining the target market for your tourist destination, detailing the market's needs and wants, and then fulfilling these needs and wants better than competitive or alternative destinations.[2] To help simplify the planning process, we have broken it down into various steps that need to be addressed when developing a strategic marketing plan. These steps and suggestions are applicable for any city or locale.

For the purpose of helping to understand the planning process, we have created a generic location, "Your City, U.S.A." The concepts and ideas presented assume a city with a minimum population base of 50,000 and with no growth limit. Although we have created some action steps involving a fictitious locale that attracts 250,000 tourists annually and is located adjacent to a major metropolitan city, this plan can be modified by substituting steps that are more appropriate to your city's specific circumstances, such as if your city or town is located near a body of water. Various sections of the book address this unique feature in the planning process. The scenario presented herein can be tailored to your location by using the suggested process and the work forms included in Part Two of this book.

Before we begin a suggested strategic marketing plan for Your City, let's briefly look at the major action steps, which we referred to earlier, that we will follow for the suggested planning process (see Table 1).

TABLE 1. Contents of the Strategic Planning Process

Preface
Executive Summary
Competitive and Environmental Assessment
Mission Statement
Goals and Objectives
Strategies and Tactics
Driving Forces
  • Environment/Perceptions
  • Metropolis/Your City attractions
  • Room Nights/Revenue
Tourism and Marketing Weaponry
  • Promotions
  • Advertising
  • Co-Ops
  • Sales
  • Events
  • Public Relations
Recommendations
The Vision
Slogans
Issues
Measurements and Results
Budget
The Appendix

PART ONE:
THE STRATEGIC TOURISM
MARKETING PLAN

THE PREFACE

The first step in the marketing plan is the Preface, which is an introductory statement that briefly delineates what the document is all about or what to expect. Let's look now at the sample preface for Your City.

PREFACE

This strategic tourism marketing plan contains many recommendations for Your City, from a mission statement to specific tactics that provide both generators of revenue and environmental improvements. Its focus is strategic, covering the next three to five years with respect to the overall tourist market, as well as tactical, in that it addresses more immediate action steps to increase returns in the current and subsequent fiscal years. The strategic and tactical elements should be viewed as interlinked, and to a large extent, they are by-products of each other.

Overall, the strategies and tactics, while seeking to generate revenue, are based on the premise of improving and preserving the community, its appeal, and its attractiveness. The environmental and competitive assessment highlights its strengths, weaknesses, opportunities, and threats. The mission statement suggests an overall vision for Your City that, once agreed upon, should be the focal point upon which future actions are based.

Finally, this strategic marketing plan should be realistic in its application of resources, focus of attention, and recommended action steps. It suggests specific ways to achieve its goals and objectives either from an operation and manpower methodology or a resource allocation perspective. It strongly urges coordination, cooperation, and communication to support the achievement of its mission.

EXECUTIVE SUMMARY

Following the Preface, the written plan should move on to the Executive Summary. This is the key to presenting, communicating, and convincing busy government and corporate community leaders to pay attention and to read on. The executive summary should articulate the organization's mission statement, goals and objectives, strategies and tactics, as well as address issues and highlight the planning document's recommendations. Let's examine a typical executive summary for Your City's plan.

EXECUTIVE SUMMARY

An environmental and competitive assessment of the strengths, weaknesses, opportunities, and threats reveals a crossroads in terms of tourism for Your City. The overall ingredients for Your City's success are based in the assets of the community, yet the accumulation of weaknesses and threats can disrupt the status quo. A major downturn at one of Your City's largest employers and the incremental deterioration of the visual environment and Your City's infrastructure are potential and real threats.

In summary, Your City is at that 50 to 60 percent threshold, where it can secure its position as a "destination within a destination," or it can struggle to maintain its current status quo. The recommendations contained in this tourism marketing plan focus on the former option.

At this point in time, and for the duration of the plan's five-year period, the following mission statement is appropriate:

> Your City seeks to enhance its overall environment by providing for the broadening of its economic base, newly generated revenues and growth through tourism, and related infrastructure development that complements its residential attractiveness.

Tourism marketing, infrastructure, and new economic development needs to be targeted as an action plan to offset pending attraction-related economic declines. A reasonable goal to strive for is a 7 to 10 percent annual growth, measured in revenues, during the planning period.

Five objectives have been identified to address this goal:

1. Enhance the overall environment, both physically and perceptually.
2. Broaden the economic base while providing for new revenues.
3. Develop the infrastructure to be visitor friendly and to increase the length of visitors' stays.
4. Maximize resources for tourism marketing.

5. Improve communications to all audiences, including the marketing realm, the public, and local residents.

In order to achieve these objectives, three primary driving forces need to be addressed in the focal points of the strategy: (1) change the initial visual perception of Your City's overall tourism environment; (2) increase cooperation and synergy with the nearby attraction's marketing efforts; and (3) maximize the focus of marketing expenditures on promotional offers to produce room-related revenues.

To address these driving forces, this plan suggests the full use of all marketing weaponry—promotions, advertising, cooperatives, sales, events, and public relations—to work in synergy with the overall goal of revenue generation. Related strategies and tactics for each category of weaponry are suggested within the plan.

Further, the objectives are supported with over forty specific recommendations; some require immediate attention, and others are to be implemented during the planning period. Also presented are four budget planning approaches. Highlights from these recommendations include:

- selecting a vision or theme for the future (two are suggested for selection);
- optional concepts to immediately improve the poor first impression by tourists of Your City's infrastructure;
- potential development concepts to provide an additional attraction for Your City, while broadening the economic base;
- infrastructure improvements to increase tourists' length of stay and to create a more "visitor friendly" Your City;
- utilization of a full-service advertising agency and public relations agency or a full-time tourism marketing coordinator;
- a promotions and events calendar;
- a public relations and communications strategy; and
- a specific cooperative opportunity.

This marketing plan strongly urges Your City to develop its own identity or "draw" through the selection and communication of a vision or theme. Two such themes and appropriate support-ing slogans are presented for discussion.

Six primary issues emerge for decision making: (1) The need for a full-time marketing/tourism function or an advertising and public relations agency; (2) the selection of Your City's vision or theme; (3) the need for new and related economic development; (4) an immediate plan for infrastructure items related to Your City's visual perception; (5) improving communications; and (6) consid-eration of a 7 percent versus a 5 percent room occupancy tax.

Acting on the recommendations, reallocating budget expendi-tures, and the resolution of the previous issues should result in a measurable increase in revenues (7 percent to 10 percent on an annual basis); increased room occupancies and rates for lodging facilities; visual enhancements to the city; improved infrastruc-ture for both visitors and residents; and the preservation and potential enhancement of both residential and commercial areas within the city.

COMPETITIVE AND ENVIRONMENTAL ASSESSMENT

A section usually located in the beginning of the planning document is the Competitive and Environmental Assessment. This step provides a realistic assessment of the tourist destination's strengths and weaknesses and its surrounding opportunities and threats (commonly referred to as the SWOT analysis) and then takes a close look at its competition. A strength is an asset or a resource of your city/town that can be used to improve its competitive position, such as an amusement park, a new medical complex, or a strong retail base. A weakness is just the opposite—a resource or capability that may cause your city/town to have a less competitive position, which can adversely affect tourism. For instance, empty commercial space or vacant buildings are categorized as weaknesses. Opportunities are developed from a tourist destination's strengths, or set of positive circumstances, and can include tourist overflow from a nearby metropolitan city or the opportunity for special events within your city/town. Threats are viewed as problems that focus on your weaknesses and which can create a potentially negative situation. Depressed commercial activity or a competing tourist destination's growing summer music festival are some examples of threats.

Often it is helpful to take a multidimensional analytical perspective in this step of the process: first examine the surrounding areas, and then imagine the future, or project what is likely to occur in your surroundings. Let's now view the environmental and competitive assessment for Your City.

COMPETITIVE AND ENVIRONMENTAL ASSESSMENT

Your City's tourism and marketing plan strategies should be based on a realistic assessment of the area's environmental and competitive position. This assessment should include a factual SWOT (strengths, weaknesses, opportunities, and threats) analysis that is both objective and subjective in nature. The perspective should also include looking around at your competition, looking within at Your City itself, and looking ahead to the next five years.

Strengths: Looking around, Your City's key strengths include its proximity to a metropolitan city and its area attraction with an annual draw of 250,000 visitors, both of which are major tourism infrastructure strengths. Another strength is its specific layout that naturally separates its residential community from its commercial industry. Certainly, Your City's attractive residential area, with its natural greenery, well-maintained homes, and landscaping, is another asset. Center islands, seasonal banners, and an overall clean appearance create a favorable impression on both residents and tourists. The location of the Your City's commercial development in relation to the visitor traffic flow is also good. The fact that the city's attractions require travel through the city itself is also an asset with respect to potential incremental revenue production. Your City's infrastructure, which includes several lodging facilities with different room rates, a recognized hospital, and an ample array of restaurants, adds to the city's list of strengths. As mentioned earlier, the overall location of Your City, situated adjacent to a major metropolitan city and near its numerous attractions, is a key strength, but it also represents a weakness, as Your City is not actually located in the major activity center.

From a tourist's perspective, Your City has the potential to be a more attractive enclave, despite its location within a general area having a number of unattractive elements. In other words, Your City appears to be two-thirds of the way toward being rated very attractive, yet this situation could easily be reversed by the numerous potential threats and real weaknesses within the city.

Weaknesses: Your city's thoroughfare, leading to and from the nearby metropolis, and its subsequent traffic flow problems is a drawback—although not of such magnitude as to be overwhelming. Another very visible weakness is the surrounding cosmetics of the major thoroughfare from the area attraction. The lack of greenery, landscaping, and positive visual impressions cause tourists to think, "let's leave" soon after visiting the attraction. Likewise, although there are area attractions in Your City, none stand out or are so popular as to result in an overnight stay by visitors.

In viewing the city, a tourist does not realize that the negative visible aspects of the main routes from the metropolitan city are not part of Your City. In fact, a visitor draws the opposite conclusion: "Why doesn't Your City clean this up?" This deterrent to tourists staying to shop and partake in other activities is further reinforced by the vacant commercial space. Although the existing seasonal banners and landscaping are a significant visual asset, they need to be extended to this roadway, visitors have no reason to be drawn into the attractiveness of Your City.

In most resort and tourist area studies, the number one factor that encourages incremental revenue, length of visit, and overnight stays is shopping availability—particularly women's boutiques and specialty shops. Your City lacks packaging, or a visual lead-in to attract visitors to its shopping areas, and is in need of both a different mix of shops and additional boutiques and specialty shops. Signs and general directions to these shops, other attractions, and parking areas could be vastly improved, particularly along Your City's main roadway.

In summary, there is no single overriding weakness in Your City. However, the combination of the aforementioned factors leads to a negative perception by tourists and local residents and reinforces the need to focus on improving the city's supporting infrastructure.

There are other areas of concern that should be noted—most important, a major lack of communication and coordination among all parties involved in promoting and marketing Your City. Also, although the city manager has done an admirable job of focusing on tourism and marketing, however, the job of marketing tourism is complex and should merit a full-time person. (Refer to the budget recommendations discussed later in the marketing plan.)

Opportunities: In its excellent lodging and food and beverage facilities, Your City has three significant opportunities to increase revenues. However, its overall opportunity is to "image up," or to change its visual perception to enhance everything in the city from room rates to real estate values. A second opportunity is infrastructure development, meaning more stores and retail outlets, improved signs, etc., to increase both the length of visitors' stays and revenues for the city. Yet another opportunity, and one with a high potential return, is to address the need for the full-time coordination of marketing efforts while capitalizing on "co-ops," or the joining with other companies to advertise, thus sharing in the associated costs. Not only will this stretch Your City's marketing dollars, it will also improve returns, either through an increased number of visitors and overnight stays or improved revenues. Other opportunities for Your City with respect to its marketing include more aggressive promotional offers; the creation and redirection of special events to generate increased room-related revenues and less traffic; other cooperative efforts; multiple public relations tie-ins and focuses; and more effective and efficient advertising. All of these recommendations will be discussed in greater detail in the strategies and tactics section of the marketing plan.

By focusing on these opportunities along with improved marketing tactics, Your City will have the overall opportunity to become its own "destination within a destination." Moreover, Your City will have the chance to position itself in a true enclave status, moving from its current two-thirds level on a teetering pendulum to the 100 percent level in its market. Over the next five years, Your City has the opportunity to become known as "the place," not only within its local surrounding communities and the adjacent metropolis, but also within its state, region, and potentially the nation. The results of these efforts will be an enhanced revenue base and increased real estate values—a win-win situation for Your City.

Threats: "Why capitalize on our opportunities, when we can just maintain the status quo?" The answer is quite simple—the status quo is quickly changing and has the potential to take a turn for the worse. Initially, there are several megathreats to address. First, one of Your City's largest employers has recently announced cutbacks and potential layoffs. This will most likely lead to a doubling of "for sale" signs in residential areas as a result of lost jobs, early retirements, and job transfers, thus creating the perception of a declining residential real estate market. Second, a decline in goods and services sold at local establishments will most likely cause some to cease operation, resulting in a greater number of empty commercial buildings, fueling even more negative perceptions. Overall, as the potential for a declining corporate base increases, fewer business transactions will take place and commercial interest will decline. Business travelers will likely seek lodging in either more attractive or alternate locations, which translates into fewer visitors and overnight stays and less revenue. Protecting Your City's corporate base as well as its leisure markets is important to forestall this snowball effect.

Thus, there is a need to accelerate the development of Your City as a tourist destination in itself. To ensure competitiveness in the battle for a share of the tourism market, there is a need to spend existing marketing dollars effectively and efficiently while developing a proactive public relations program. Currently, Your City's lodging facilities are well-positioned, well-maintained, and well-operated. If their surroundings start to deteriorate, their competitive position weakens substantially. This, combined with the plethora of new budget and limited service hotels lining the roadway from the major metropolitan city, could become a major threat to Your City's room revenues and subsequent tax generation.

In summary, it is unlikely that the current environmental and competitive situation of Your City will remain the status quo. These threats should be responded to with the appropriate degree of urgency.

THE MISSION STATEMENT

The core of the actual marketing planning document begins with the Mission Statement, which is a concise narrative statement summarizing your organization's objectives and ultimate goals. It provides a clear direction for everyone working in your organization, serves as a basis for communication, asserts a philosophy for doing business, and provides a basis for evaluating your organization.[3] In essence, a mission statement outlines why you are in business. Now let's view the mission statement for Your City.

MISSION STATEMENT

A mission statement represents the end result of your objectives as well as the achievement of your ultimate goals, while defining what your organization is all about. Once agreed upon, it becomes the benchmark against which all strategies and human and financial resource allocations are measured. Furthermore, a mission statement is a communications vehicle, whose purpose is to be clear, concise, and directional while focusing on the planning period as well as the future. This plan suggests a mission statement for Your City that ultimately is the end product of the leadership in its community.

> Your City seeks to enhance its overall environment by broadening its economic base and providing newly generated revenues and growth through tourism and related infrastructure development that complements its residential attractiveness.

GOALS AND OBJECTIVES

The next step, which immediately follows the mission statement, is the section entitled Goals and Objectives. Goals are both qualitative and quantitative, which means that they are comprised of both data-based estimates and educated guesses, although realistic estimates are preferred.[4] Objectives outline what needs to be accomplished during the time frame of the plan. They must be specific, measurable in a quantifiable manner, related to a specific time period, and focused on affecting the behavior of your destination's tourist market. Let's now look at the goals and objectives for Your City.

GOALS AND OBJECTIVES

Although the overall goal is the fulfillment of Your City's mission statement, a realistic and quantifiable goal should be:

> To seek to offset pending economic declines (as a minimum target) with the achievement of actual growth through tourism development at an annualized rate of up to 10 percent (in terms of revenue) during the plan's duration.

Reaching this goal would be based upon the achievement of the following primary objectives:

1. Enhance Your City's overall environment, both physically and perceptually.
2. Broaden the economic base while providing for new revenues.
3. Develop Your City's infrastructure to be visitor friendly and to increase the length of visitors' stays.
4. Maximize resources for tourism marketing.
5. Improve communications to all audiences, including the marketing realm, the public, and local residents.

Each of these primary objectives is supported with a set of strategies and tactics for their implementation in the next section of this plan.

Driving Forces

It is important to recognize that there are three major driving forces in the Your City's situation which are of such magnitude that they need to be discussed individually from the strategic issues. These driving forces, although interrelated to a large degree, should be viewed both individually and collectively.

Driving Force #1: Environmental Perceptions

It has often been said that an initial visual perception sets the stage for everything else. Unfortunately, Your City's major roadway conveys the initial impression to its tourists that this is not a place to stay, shop, dine, and be entertained. This needs to be addressed immediately, as it does not encourage visitors to venture beyond their trip to the nearby attraction. This negative perception is further reinforced by the absence of any positive "Welcome to Your City" image—in the form of landscaping, signs, fountains, or archways. In addition, an abundance of "for lease/sale" signs and vacant commercial buildings only add to the overall negative image. Tourists do not get the impression that "Your City is attractive, charming, and well worth a visit or an overnight stay." As a result, they remain close-minded to the well-maintained streets of Your City and its seasonal banners and other amenities. This negative driving force needs both immediate and long-term attention—*it is significant enough to depress room rates, discourage overnight stays, deter visitors from shopping, and reduce both commercial and residential real estate values.* Action needs to be taken to change tourists' initial visual perceptions of Your City.

Driving Force #2: The Attraction/Metropolis Area

The nearby attraction represents the "magnet" that draws over 250,000 visitors to the road that fronts Your City. Recognizing, embracing, and cooperating with this attraction in all areas will result in a win-win situation for both parties.

Multiple opportunities exist to achieve both incremental and new revenues as well as improved marketing efficiencies as a result of a close working relationship with the attraction's marketing department. Although specific recommendations are explained in detail later in this plan, some key areas of improvement include joint promotions; exit and entrance signs; room and admissions packages; event coordination; co-ops of every type and variety; environment and perception improvements; and group sales coordination. *It is not unreasonable for Your City to target and achieve a 7 to 10 percent increase in overnight stays and revenue from these efforts.* As important as it is to have Your City mentioned in all of the adjacent metropolitan city's newspapers, trade publications, magazines, and other advertising channels, *the priority is to focus on bringing in overnight visitors and increasing their length of stay.* Although specific recommendations will be detailed in the promotional and advertising components of this strategic plan, it is strongly suggested that Your City focus its marketing dollars on promotions that include room packages in Your City. The proximity and major draw of the area attraction is a great asset to Your City and represents a potentially strong marketing partner for the future.

Driving Force #3: Room Nights and Revenues

What better way to increase revenues than to increase both room rates and room nights at Your City's lodging facilities. Overnight guests create multiple revenue generation opportunities in the form of rooms, food and beverage, retail sales, and admission fees. *The strategic opportunity here is to focus marketing expenditures on promotional offers, events, and other specific actions that produce room sales and/or higher room rates.*

In summary, these three driving forces should be the strategic focal points for the tourism marketing strategies, tactics, action plans, and recommendations. This does not imply that public relations may cease to focus on Your City's image or that activities involving informational brochures or other collateral materials need be abandoned. Rather, it clearly prioritizes how marketing dollars and resources should be allocated.

STRATEGIES AND TACTICS

The next step of the strategic tourism marketing plan focuses on how the goals and objectives as previously outlined will now be achieved. This section is called the Strategies and Tactics section of the planning process. Strategies are simply action plans that detail how the marketing variables of product, price, place, and promotion (commonly referred to as the four Ps of marketing)[5] are used to attain the plan's annual objectives and overall strategies.

The first "P," product, explains the existing products or services offered, as well as any future changes to be made to the products or services, packaging, and their physical design. A product can be tangible, e.g., a city, a store or a piece of furniture, or it can be intangible, e.g., the service a guest receives from a hotel and its staff.

The second "P," price, outlines pricing strategies to be used and the rationale behind them. Pricing objectives can be based on profit or sales maximization or to enhance market share. Various strategies used can include market penetration, bundling products, or reacting to competitive price changes.[6]

The third "P," place, includes all factors relating to the distribution channels of the product or service to the customer. Areas that are addressed in the distribution plan include market penetration, types of channels, competition, geography, and timing.[7]

Finally, the last "P," promotions, refers to any activities that stimulate and create consumer interest in a particular product or service.[8] These activities may include special events, offers, exhibits, or discounts through the use of advertising, sales, public relations, and publicity.

In addition, the Strategies and Tactics section clearly discusses the tactics involved—specific items or steps needed to implement the marketing strategies. It is also in this section that specific marketing techniques are covered—often referred to as the application of marketing weaponry or tools. Let's now look at the strategies and tactics for Your City.

STRATEGIES AND TACTICS

Having previously identified the driving forces behind the plan's strategies and tactics, the following are specific tourism and marketing strategies based on the weaponry of six marketing techniques. These marketing techniques that will produce maximum returns include promotions, advertising, co-ops, sales, events, and public relations. Each one plays a significant role independently as well as in support of the others.

Promotions

A revolving promotional calendar will be implemented utilizing either a ninety-day or quarterly time-frame (refer to the detailed promotional calendar in Figure 1 later in this section). Wherever possible, the use of win-win cooperative efforts will prove to be the most effective. Also, a variety of promotions is suggested for both base-level or ongoing promotions and special event promotions. The following base-level promotions will perform well in increasing overnight stays:

PROMO #1: Kids Are Free

This promotion is targeted toward the leisure market segment and is aimed at taking room occupancy market share from other adjacent metropolitan markets. The basic promotion will have the following promise: Kids Are Free—Stay overnight at Your City's lodging facilities and your kids will not only stay for free and eat for free, but they will also receive free admission to the area attraction. A disclaimer will be required outlining the following: based on regular rack room rates or as determined by individual establishments; based on limited room availability; children must be accompanied by adults; one free meal and complementary attraction ticket per child (maximum two children per room); the free meal must be from the children's menu; and the promotion applies to children twelve years old and under. The promotion will require a cooperative effort with the attraction to receive the best or lowest rate on children's admission ticket prices, and the participating lodging facilities would be required to understand the economics involved in offering the promotion during a lower demand period at a proper price. *Nevertheless, the incentive is sufficiently attractive to entice visitors to select Your City's lodging facilities and will fill empty rooms, take market share, and produce revenue.*

The promotion's target markets, considered to be a group of people or organizations that have a common set of characteristics, include feeder cities (main cities within a geographic region that tend to feed travel to each other)[9] in the home state and in bordering states. A version of this concept may also be utilized for the special leisure group sales market. It is important to recognize that the strongest hook of the Kids Are Free promotion is the word "free," and the greatest perceived value is the admission ticket to the attraction. However, each component of the promotion may be adjusted based on the perspectives of individual establishments.

PROMO #2: Stay and Save

This promotion works for both the leisure and business markets. The promotion is as follows: Stay overnight in Your City and receive a dollar amount discount or a percentage discount at these stores, restaurants, and events with your Stay and Save Card. The key is to aim for either a minimum of a 10 percent discount or offer different levels of percentages based on the length of stay. For instance, group A, which represents travelers that stay at the hotel for one night, receives a 10 percent discount; group B, or travelers that stay three nights, receives a 15 percent discount; group C, or travelers that stay five nights, receives a 25 percent discount, etc. The stores used in the promotion could be in Your City as well as at the area attraction or the local shopping mall. An alternate concept could be an actual booklet of savings in dollar amounts. For example, for a one-night stay, a visitor would receive a $5 coupon; for a two-night stay, they would receive a $10 coupon. This, similar to the discount percentage offer, is at no cost to the lodging facilities, as the merchants themselves set the parameters involved. This promotion will be aimed at both the in-state market and neighboring states, as well as the international tourist market.

PROMO #3: Stay and Play

This promotion, which is aimed at the leisure market, uses a coupon booklet of discounts at area attractions coupled with an overnight stay in Your City. The perception of value is established in the minds of the visitors by including a pitch or message that the booklet "contains over $500.00 in savings." Other target markets for this promotion include the in-state leisure segment and visitors from nearby states.

PROMO #4: Seniors Free

This statewide promotion is aimed at seniors and provides free admission to the area attraction, along with a coupon booklet for discounts at area shops and restaurants. However, only one free admission ticket is entitled per overnight stay. The seniors market is a significant one, and this promotion needs to be a priority in the upcoming year. Expansion to markets outside of the state can also be implemented.

PROMO #5: Your City Gift Club

This promotion is a builder of repeat business and is aimed at the business segment. It involves a points program in which, for each overnight stay or a certain dollar amount spent at a Your City lodging facility, a business traveler earns a certificate or point value toward a premium gift from Your City merchants or possibly the area attraction's gift shop. Of course, selection and value amounts will be determined by the cooperating hotels, who in turn reimburse the merchants for the gifts. Be sure to target the business traveler who stays overnight in the metropolitan area and travels the next day on business in Your City's vicinity.

PROMO #6: Shop and Save

Here a booklet or discount card that contains discounts and other offers from various merchants in Your City will be given out ree of charge to paying visitors to the area's attractions. This will act as a local revenue generator by encouraging a longer length of stay by visitors. Awareness of retail outlets is increased and is tied into an incentive to shop and save in Your City.

PROMO #7: Events and Group Related

This promotion involves working in conjunction with both the attraction and its surrounding area as well as Your City's planned events and special groups. Here, an incentive will be offered for visitors to "stay another day" in Your City. Details of the offer will be selected by the participating lodging facilities and merchants.

In summary, strong promotional offers are needed to improve the existing 60 to 70 percent room occupancy rates in Your City, U.S.A. The following promotional calendar (see Figure 1) provides a timetable for an ongoing series of promotions aimed at improving room revenues and increasing market share to entice a greater number of the area attraction's annual 250,000 visitors to become overnight guests and patrons of Your City's retail merchants. Additional promotional ideas are outlined in The Appendix and Recommendations sections of this plan.

Advertising

The strategic focal points that relate to Your City's advertising strategy focus on three key areas: (1) creative, (2) media selection and mix, and (3) target markets. It is important to remember that advertising refers to that which informs and persuades your visitors through paid media, or vehicles of communication—television, radio, magazine, newspaper, outdoor, and direct mail.[10] Each of the components of the advertising strategy is addressed in the following material.

Creative

Advertising creative, or the development of creative and communicative advertising, should be driven by promotions. Image advertising, whose aim is to develop an enduring brand identity,

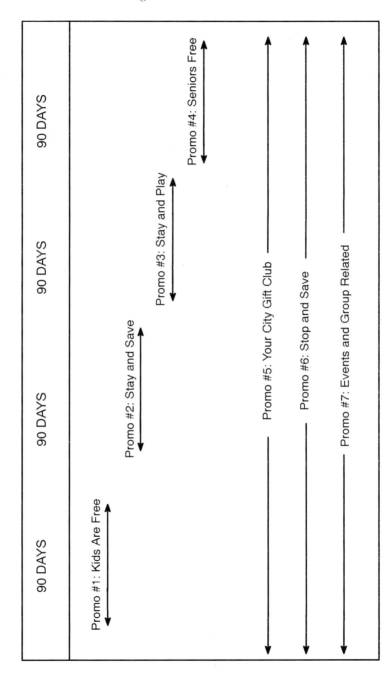

FIGURE 1. Promotional Calendar

is best left to the other marketing weapons, particularly public relations. Your City needs a greater number of visitors to stay overnight as well as additional room revenues to fill its valley periods. In our consumer-oriented promotional environment, where decisions are often based upon the best offer or most value, virtually all advertising needs to have its creative message include a promotional offer (with the exception of listings and directories). Although the photo selection and the slogan used in advertising can convey a particular image, *the advertising creative must emphasize a promotional offer and wherever possible create a coupon or tear-out discount.*

Media Selection and Mix

The key to a successful advertising campaign is to select the most effective, efficient, and affordable medium. Here, due to the relative size of Your City's advertising budget and its selected target markets, *print-based media should be utilized.* Since the advertising effort supports the promotional offers previously discussed, feeder city newspapers in major cities within the state and local suburban areas, regional magazines, and selected in-flight airline publications should be used. Also AAA and AARP publications should be reviewed, particularly when event promotions are advertised.

The use of direct mail to selected lists of visitors is another component in the media selection process. For example, utilize American Express and VISA charge cards lists of business travelers to Your City's area to create a direct mail list. Cooperative opportunities with the media, credit card companies, and the area attraction should be taken advantage of. In fact, taking advantage of the attraction's greater buying power and media discounts or those of the metropolis's Convention and Visitors Bureau could prove to be very economical.

Target Markets

Your City should focus on the area attraction's markets as its primary target markets as well as corporate target markets specified by local hotels. Fine-tuning any available data about Your City's visitors will make efforts in targeting your markets more efficient. For instance, 20 percent of visitors to Your City are international—this suggests that Your City's promotions, such as Shop and Save, be targeted (perhaps cooperatively between the hotels, merchants, and the city) at these international markets and their intermediaries (travel agencies, tour operators, etc.). Refer to Tables 2 and 3 for more information about visitors to Your City.

TABLE 2. Origin of Visitors to Your City—Global Markets

65%	In State
20%	International
15%	Other States in the United States

TABLE 3. Top Five International Markets for Your City

1.	Canada
2.	Mexico
3.	Germany
4.	France
5.	Japan

Co-Ops

Your City has opportunities to significantly stretch its marketing budget through tie-ins and cooperative efforts with partners of greater size and reach. Here are some potential opportunities to be explored:

The Area's Attraction

This co-op offers multiple beneficial cooperative opportunities including signs, exchange of promotional booklets, interlinked promotional offers, events and group sales programs, cooperative advertising, joint direct mail, cross promotions, as well as greater clout when approaching vendors, the state, and others.

Regional and National Airline Carriers

These co-ops offer targeted media opportunities as well as group desk activities, potential direct mail inclusions, leads on groups visiting the area, and potential sales cooperation (contacting agents and tour operators for both domestic and international business).

Events-Related Activities

Such activities that support the marketing plan's objectives of generating room nights and additional revenue could prove beneficial in cooperative efforts. One way to confirm this support is to determine whether cooperatively contributing to this actually generates room nights and revenue and whether Your City would already receive this benefit without such a cooperative fund allocation. Another approach to cooperative events suggests that Your City be the location for the event that generates room nights as well as cooperatively creating these events with interest groups, additional sponsors, and clubs. (This will be explained in greater detail in the Events part of this section and also in the Recommendations section.)

Other Attractions

Additional attractions in Your City can be pursued in cooperatives only if needed. For instance, a close relationship with a metropolitan shopping mall might generate promotional ties or even fill an empty Your City store with an annex shop from one of the mall's retailers. Also, discounts for inclusion in promotional offers can often result from a strong relationship with nearby merchants.

Sales

Your City and its lodging establishments can benefit from cooperative sales efforts—joining with other companies to sell their

products and services. Selling created events and soliciting annual or periodic events can also be beneficial. Working cooperatively with the area attraction for corporate weekend events can be beneficial in valley or low weekend periods. Consider tying these weekends to corporate account incentive programs or human resource company-wide events. Group sales efforts within each lodging facility should work closely with the attraction to complement its booked events and at the same time explore opportunities for win-win situations with corporate customers. For example, a Your City hotel in competition with a non–Your City hotel for a piece of group business may win the business by holding a reception at the attraction. Likewise, perhaps Your City could be the actual "theme" event packaged for a particular group. Other cooperative sales efforts include contacting bus tour operators, hosting seniors and various school tours and excursions. Likewise, themed weekends where Your City is the destination can be developed and targeted toward other states' towns and cities for birthdays, historic events, anniversaries, themed sports weekends, and club weekends (for example, auto clubs and hobby clubs).

Events

Events can be solicited and developed to focus on the marketing plan's objectives of generating room nights and additional revenue. Event marketing, sometimes referred to as event sponsorship, is a rapidly growing area due to its success in cutting through advertising clutter while reaching target markets with great effect.[11] Examples of such events include an award function, a weekend meeting of a classic car club with a planned afternoon function, a telethon, a street festival, a walk-a-thon, or a theater and arts-related weekend. These events should be solicited, developed, and, where possible, utilized with cooperative concepts.

A proposed series of events throughout a specific period of time, often referred to as an event calendar, can generate attention and revenue for Your City. A proposed events calendar is as follows:

January (and Ongoing)

The Your City Bridge-A-Thon will be held statewide as a bridge tournament for senior citizens. A weekend competition will be held monthly as points accumulate throughout the year until a winner is crowned in the final weekend of December.

February

The Annual Your City Barbershop Competition is a weekend event developed in concert with the Society for the Preservation of Barbershop Quartet Singing in America (SPBQSA) with chapters nationwide.

March Through May

Your City's Area Attraction Festival featuring special music concerts with popular bands, rides, and an attractive carnival-like display entertains visitors of all ages. For communities that border a local body of water, a paddle boat competition sponsored by the community's principal hospitality entities could be staged.

April

The Your City 10K Annual Race is intended to benefit a worthy cause such as the American Red Cross. Corporate sponsors should be sought.

May

The Your City Flower Festival features a blend of internationally acclaimed horticultural gardens and local artisans and artists.

June

Your City's International Food Extravaganza is a weekend event with participating hotels and restaurants in the Your City

and metropolitan city area. For communities near a body of water, an annual City Cups competition for fishermen could be structured for different age categories.

July

Your City hosts the annual Fourth of July weekend extravaganza.

August

The Your City Street Festival is a weekend event promoting the city's rich cultural history, and the highlight is a street dance with local musicians and bands.

September

The Your City Art Event is an annual weekend event with sponsorship from the local art gallery and museums that will be a good draw for the Labor Day weekend. Exhibits for visitors of all ages will be displayed. For communities that border a body of water, a boatbuilding competition where the water worthiness of each entry is demonstrated is also appropriate.

October

An Antique Show and Auction will involve both local residents and visitors from throughout the state.

November

The Rolls Royce Rendezvous—a weekend gathering of these elite cars from throughout the state and beyond would include a parade and a display of cars and competitions for prizes, with an award banquet at the end of the weekend.

December

A Christmas Parade or Annual Tree Lighting Ceremony involving local lodging establishments is appropriate. If your communi-

ty is located near a body of water, a Christmas Boat Parade can also be staged.

Public Relations

This section presents a series of proposed public relations initiatives, yet another marketing tool that is a communications vehicle between Your City and its current and potential customers. These initiatives are intended to promote significantly greater public awareness, with an enhanced public perception of Your City as a desirable destination for both business and leisure travelers.

Your City News Bureau

A city news bureau should be established to furnish a steady flow of newsworthy information about Your City to local and regional media, primarily in state as well as neighboring states. The key is to consistently communicate what is happening in the community to achieve top-of-mind awareness of Your City as an entertainment, recreational, and weekend getaway option with its own inherent appeal.

It is important to extend the reach of news messages beyond the metropolitan city area to significantly boost the percentage of visitor traffic from more distant locations. Primary international markets can also be targeted in accordance with the visitor statistics.

News releases are announcements of current newsworthy events that are of interest to the public and/or to particular groups. Issue at least one news release per week to ensure added exposure of Your City and impose the discipline necessary to develop news material on a regular basis. The content of this news is drawn from the community's hotels, restaurants, and shops participating in the community's promotions; from Your City's Convention and Visitors Bureau; and from Your City's Chamber of Commerce and its major attraction. This will be a win-win situation for all parties involved as so many elements of Your City's hospitality industry's infrastructure are participating.

Promotions such as the suggested Kids Are Free, Stay and Save, Stay and Play, and Seniors Free, as well as special events centered on cultural, entertainment, and recreational activities are typical examples of news releases subjects. Community image enhancement projects can also be spotlighted, as well as other civic efforts reflecting Your City's determination to be a distinctive destination. Joint news releases with a primary entity such as the major area attraction should also be pursued to capitalize on the attraction's broad appeal.

Through a continuous and concentrated effort, this communication initiative can be accomplished at a modest cost through the use of freelance writers or other professionals who will supply the requisite expertise without the need for Your City to retain a communications professional on a full-time basis.

Press Kit

A press kit for Your City is an appropriate component for its public relations efforts. Press kits are communication folders usually comprised of two pockets—the left used for background information about the newsworthy event and the right used for press releases.[9] A comprehensive press kit containing current information about Your City's hospitality facilities, visitor attractions, and other points of distinction will demonstrate the community's appeal to a wide range of customers. The information should be periodically updated for both accuracy and freshness.

In addition to its use with the news media, the press kit itself or selected components can be distributed to a wide range of prospective business sources. It can be an excellent sales tool for Your City in a variety of ways. Press kits are useful when calling on prospective groups to interest them in holding their meetings in Your City. The press kit is also an excellent direct mail inclusion for local hotels and attractions to use in conjunction with their marketing efforts.

Monthly Newsletter

A newsletter published on a monthly basis that communicates news about Your City is another valuable tool to garner publicity.

The newsletter can be distributed to news media, travel agents, tour operators, corporations that are current or potential sources of business for Your City, and other audiences.

The publication will be a single sheet (printed on both sides) with its content drawn from information about various hospitality entities and attractions of the Your City area. This is an excellent tool for providing information for people who are in a position to produce business for Your City. A network of representatives from hotels, restaurants, attractions, and shops in the community can be created to serve as the source of the timely and critical information worthy of inclusion in the newsletter.

Press Trips

An ongoing series of press trips, primarily focused on weekend time frames, is another component of the public relations plan. Primary targets include regional newspaper travel editors and freelance writers with ties to consumer and travel trade publications. Press trips are a successful means of introducing a community, its facilities, and its attractions to journalists, who in turn communicate these messages to their readers.

These media initiatives are conducted on a complimentary basis, excluding incidental expenses incurred by the journalists such as hotel gift shop purchases and long distance phone calls. The cooperation and support of hotel, restaurants, and area attractions is necessary to make these initiatives as productive as possible. Contact regional and national airlines for gratis air transportation to eliminate the single biggest expense of the press trip.

Media Tours

These represent another productive component that generates publicity for Your City. A media tour consists of a series of concentrated meetings with selected news media representatives in a single location over a short period of time. The majority of media tours conducted on behalf of Your City can be accomplished in one to two days, given the smaller regional markets that constitute the core of the target lists. Primary expenses related to such efforts are travel, lodging, and meals for the public relations professional.

Speakers Bureau

A Speakers Bureau is a means of communicating the nature and overall appeal of the area at virtually no cost. Targets for this project are service and seniors organizations, church and women's groups, and other similar organizations located throughout a selected regional area. Many organizations of this type are eager to include interesting presentations in their regular meetings.

A slide presentation and an accompanying script is required for this purpose. A packaged presentation approximately fifteen minutes in length is easy to develop and requires little preparation time on the part of the speaker. Volunteer speakers can be solicited from within the area's hospitality industry—hotel general managers and marketing directors, restaurant operators, attraction executives, and others are well suited for such a role.

RECOMMENDATIONS

Now that the strategic tourism marketing plan detail has been outlined, it is time to provide specific recommendations for both a short- and long-term perspective. Typically, these recommendations are related to the objectives previously detailed in the goals and objectives section of the plan. This interrelationship between the recommendations and objectives should permeate daily decisions and actions in a manner consistent with the long-term success of the overall strategy.[10] Once the necessary decisions are made, specific action takes place. Let's now look at the recommendations for Your City.

RECOMMENDATIONS

When assessing both the short and long term, it is helpful to view the objectives and recommendations in a timely perspective. Although an immediate set of needs must be met within the next twelve months, the broadening of Your City's economic base remains the overall priority. Keeping this balance of needs in perspective, all objectives should be delineated in year one. Some will be achievable in this first year, others in later years during the planning period, a total of five years. Although some of these recommendations can be viewed as being beyond the scope of a tourism marketing plan, they do represent important steps toward achieving Your City's overall mission and goal and therefore have been included. In addition, at the end of this section, we have suggested several possible visions or descriptive statements of Your City in the new millennium. Let's now review each objective with its related recommendations.

Objective One: Enhancement of Your City's Overall Physical and Perceptual Environment

Recommendations

- Select a theme or vision for the future (several are suggested later in this plan in The Vision section) and work toward it.
- Consider creating a visual attraction along the main thoroughfare as one of the objective's top priorities—organize a joint meeting with the area attraction, Your City, and the State Department of Transportation-Highway Maintenance to ascertain if an interim maintenance program is possible between the present periods of state maintenance. Seek bids to potentially provide such maintenance on a more frequent basis.
- Develop and implement an interim plan for a visible entryway at both ends of the center strip. Some options include landscaping, a water display, a metal archway or a high-tech metal sculpture, or other identifiers to signal the arrival to Your City.

- Determine what can be done to occupy empty commercial buildings or to screen off the visibly deserted look in that particular section—this is a top priority.
- At the same time, review the commercial parking areas near the retail shops to determine if hanging flower baskets or barrel planters would enhance their attractiveness.
- As an additional enhancement to Your City, consider planter road dividers at the major entry streets to the residential sections of the city to deter nonresident traffic (the planters act as barriers to auto traffic).

Objective Two: Broaden the Economic Base While Providing for New Revenues

Recommendations

- To broaden the economic base, consider utilizing a vacant warehouse or a commercial complex to house:

  · an exhibit facility for events that draw overnight visitors,
  · a new shopping attraction,
  · a conference center with the latest in high-tech equipment, or
  · a new cultural attraction.

- Consider the development of new facilities to provide Your City with its own attraction that can draw 250,000 visitors into the area while creating new demand:

  · an air and space museum,
  · an art and performance theater area,
  · a water park theme attraction,
  · a water life museum or aquarium, or
  · a high-tech exhibit hall.

- Explore the potential conversion of Your City's vacant buildings for alternative uses such as:

  · a movie theater—an imagination center of science fiction entertainment, with sponsorship from a major movie studio;

- a children's performing theater—on weekends and in the summers;
- Your City's Performance Hall—an evening performance center that is tied in to packages with hotels for rooms; or
- an entertainment center—for adults and children of all ages.

- Solicit a developer of an international European market center to transform the vacant commercial space into an interior courtyard facility with European shops, bakeries, flower markets, restaurants, and small offices.

Objective Three: Develop the Infrastructure to be Visitor Friendly and to Increase the Length of Visitors' Stays

Recommendations

- Implement a new, consistent, and visitor-friendly signage program utilizing a vertical sign concept to include specific community elements, e.g., medical services, shops, residential and commercial areas. Where at all possible use internationally recognized symbols.
- Seek cooperation from the area attraction to provide directional signs to the shops and restaurants of Your City at the exits of their visitors' parking areas. Develop a handout card or brochure for visitors to receive at the attraction.
- Intensify efforts to attract additional shops, boutiques, and art galleries to the vacant facilities in Your City.
- Explore the possibility of a weekend or seasonal shuttle service to take visitors from the area attraction to the shops, restaurants, and lodging facilities of Your City. Theme the shuttle to the vision for Your City and consider it as an attraction in itself. For example, the shuttle could resemble a trolley or double-decker bus related to an international village concept. The service does not have to be free of charge to visitors—it can be self-supporting. In fact, the trolley or shuttle does not even need to be operative, rather it can just be parked on the Your City side of the road while acting to draw visitors to the city.

- Consider utilizing other vacant space as an artist display area or an exhibit space (e.g., for classic cars) to provide infrastructure to the city, while keeping in mind the overnight stay objective.
- Consider theming the shopping area with the Flags of the Nations, while creating an international village flavor or concept.

Objective Four: Maximize Resources for Tourism Marketing

Recommendations

- Consider utilizing a small full-service advertising and public relations agency with promotions development and related capabilities—a small agency will ensure that the Your City account is viewed as an important one. Explore the possibility of using the attraction's agencies for greater efficiency and cooperative inclusion opportunities.
- Implement the promotion calendar concept as soon as possible.
- Develop an events calendar for the new millennium.
- Seek the full application of the cooperative concept for cross-marketing purposes with the attraction and other agencies identified in this plan.
- Implement a full public relations program aimed at all of Your City's target markets in conjunction with the environmental and perceptual improvements, the new events and promotions, and the infrastructure action steps.
- Consider identifying certain time periods of either weeks or months as themed marketing periods associated with Your City's international and domestic visitors; for example, have a Canada month in Your City. Notify all travel-related business generators and use a public relations program to generate interest.
- Identify and solicit various clubs (e.g., auto, hobby), associations, and organizations for multiple room night-related events and meetings in Your City. Coordinate your efforts with the group sales functions, the attraction's marketing arm, and Your City's Convention and Visitors Bureau.

- Explore a unique billboard concept for Your City or the main thoroughfare from the adjacent metropolitan city. The billboards can be multidimensional, inflatable, or movement oriented.
- Consider a cooperative billboard at the adjacent airport for Your City's hotels.
- Review opportunities to have Your City become a prize destination for a free trip in a television show targeted to your audiences. Seek airline partners to provide transportation to ensure that the television exposure is given to the participating hotels.

Objective Five: Improve Communications to All Audiences, Including the Marketing Realm, the Public, and Local Residents

Recommendations

- Consider allocating resources toward the creation of a full-time marketing and tourism position, whose responsibilities would include coordinating cooperative marketing programs, developing and executing promotions, soliciting events, and providing communications vehicles.
- Identify the vision for Your City and then communicate it in the logo and slogan for Your City to ensure consistency.
- Establish a communications plan to keep everyone abreast of all activities to ensure a synergistic effort while maximizing efficiencies. Ensure adequate lead time is provided to everyone involved and include monthly updates, quarterly briefings, and weekly contacts.
- Review the adjacent metropolitan city's Convention and Visitors Bureau's efforts and seek to be included in their events and shows.
- Keep your residents informed of the overall tourism marketing effort and its progress with regularly scheduled meetings, mailings, and presentations. Regularly seek their input into the process and encourage residents to convey the image of a visitor-friendly or hospitable city.

- Seek to complement the area attraction's communications newsletter and where possible piggyback with a city column or paragraph.
- Ensure easy identification, directions, and clear signage for all of Your City's tourism and visitor venues.
- Seek to have newspapers in the adjacent states' feeder city markets publish releases, promotional calendar offers, events, and other news about Your City.
- Develop a Your City panel card or brochure for use by visitors and seek distribution via the area attraction and other state tourism brochure outlets.
- When ready, organize press trips for key media personnel (in particular, target print-related media) and seek favorable public relations stories.

THE VISION

In many strategic tourism marketing plans now developed, a section outlining the community's vision is often included. The Vision is a statement that vividly describes the desired outcome of the overall strategic plan. Often the section including the community's vision will present alternative scenarios for its future while providing both direction and purpose for its interim strategies and activities. Let's review a few samples for Your City.

VISION—YOUR CITY—THE NEW MILLENIUM

In order to capitalize on the benefits of tourism, Your City needs to develop its own identity. This identity or "draw" will become the focal point for its marketing weaponry, development activity, and the overall thrust of its strategic plan for the next five years. Presented are two unique concepts for this vision, each of which requires acceptance by all parties and a commitment to move forward. Although other visions are possible, each of the following alternatives was selected due to its ability to build upon Your City's existing asset base or to take advantage of the current infrastructure and economic base.

Vision One: The "Enclave" at Your City

Envision a welcoming fountain or a beautiful floral display as you enter Your City. The roads are lined with palm trees or other suitable tree plantings and surrounded with quaint art galleries, coffee shops, and boutiques. The crepe myrtles, hanging baskets, and barrel planters reflect color and warmth. Colorful festival-like banners framing the area make one say, "I want to go there, walk the streets, sip coffee, take pictures, and ride the trolley—in the enclave. Before we go back to the hotel, I want to go to the movie studio or the mall and its shops—they have great prints—it's a neat place."

This is the incomparable Your City—a trendy place for visitors and *the* place to reside.

Vision 2: The "International Village" at Your City

Envision the flags of the world's countries visible against the sky as you enter Your City, which is lined with beautiful flower beds and plantings that signal a warm welcome in any language. Glance at the exquisite-looking signs guiding you to the shopping village, restaurants, and lodging facilities, again noting the universal symbols of welcome. It must be summer festival time, as the summer banners are flying and the International Children's Theater and visiting artists are performing. In addition to the

Flags of the World Shop, there are dozens of international boutiques—full of silks, wools, and English china, along with the Bavarian restaurant, the Swiss Chocolate Shop, the English Tea Garden, and the Ice Cream Shop. Listen to the music of the roaming musicians and look, here comes the double-decker bus. What a wonderful place—a "Host to the World and Beyond." Wouldn't it be great to live here?

SLOGANS

As in many business or corporate strategic marketing plans, a city's mission, vision, goals, and objectives become reflected in the slogan. Slogans help build identity and can convey a company's position in the marketplace, which is demonstrated in the examples of "Quality Is Job One" or "The City by the Bay." They can also be created and associated with marketing campaigns, such as the campaign promoting New York City as "The Big Apple." Ultimately, a slogan becomes an image with which almost everyone in the community and its visitors can identify. Let's now take a look at some slogans for Your City.

SLOGANS

Each vision previously presented allows for an accompanying slogan. Three are presented for each vision.

Vision One Slogans: The "Enclave" at Your City

- "The Incomparable Your City"
- "The Place to Stay"
- "Enchanting Your City"

Note: The focus here is on a visual yet traditional perception of Your City.

Vision Two Slogans: "The International Village" at Your City

- "A Host to the World and Beyond"
- "A Community of the Universe"
- Any of those listed under "Vision One Slogans" are also suitable.

Note: The focus here is on a visual international and global perception of Your City.

Additional Slogans

- "Overnight or for a Lifetime"
- "Enchanting and Educational"
- "An Entertaining Place"
- "Warmth and Wonderment"
- "The Place by the Bay"

ISSUES

In the process of undertaking any strategic tourism marketing plan, several issues will surface. We recommend that these issues be collected during the planning process and set aside for appropriate discussion at the end of the actual plan. Although some issues may resolve themselves during the planning process, others may divert the process or cause delays. Addressing the issues at the end of the plan enables the community to put the issues into perspective in relation to the plan in its entirety. Let's look at the issues facing Your City.

ISSUES

A number of issues surfaced during the development of the strategic tourism marketing plan. Some have already been commented upon in various sections of the plan, predominantly in the recommendations. The issues are as follows:

- need for a full-time marketing/tourism function or an advertising and public relations agency;
- development of Your City's own identity with a distinct and unique vision, without losing the benefits associated with the area's attraction and the adjacent metropolitan city;
- need for improved communications;
- consideration of a 7 percent versus a 5 percent existing room occupancy tax rate;
- related economic development, including shops, vacant buildings, etc.; and
- related infrastructure items.

Each issue requires a separate discussion or the development of a specific solution, clearly outlining key decisions and a plan of responsibility.

MEASUREMENTS AND RESULTS

In order to ensure success, all of the activities within a strategic tourism marketing plan need to be measurable. This can be achieved in two ways—either the expected results are specific and quantifiable or they are related to key dates, milestones, or timetables. Likewise, qualitative accomplishments can be measured within time parameters or other established criteria, including polls, image assessments, or opinion surveys. Specifying these expectations is critical in determining which goals are being achieved and, as a result, whether strategies need to be modified. Let's review some key measurements and results for Your City.

MEASUREMENTS AND RESULTS

One key quantitative measurement is to offset any declines in revenues while achieving the ultimate goal *of increasing revenue an average of 7 to 10 percent on an annualized basis*. A second key measurement is to forestall any real estate value declines and to improve the perceived and real values associated with the attractiveness of Your City. A third measurable result is increasing room occupancy above the norm in competitive markets and increasing average room rates above nearby lodging competitors' rates. Finally, added value should be achieved in terms of commercial real estate draw.

Qualitatively, the measurements and results include the visible enhancements to Your City, improved infrastructure for visitors and residents, and the preservation and enhancement to both the residential and commercial areas within the city. In addition, improved communications, increased public relations efforts, and the development of a shared vision will instill a renewed sense of vitality and community that will continue to grow stronger each year.

BUDGETS

A key component of any plan is the budget allocation or planning process, as it may often seem that there are never enough marketing dollars available for the execution of the plan. Although strategic tourism marketing plans may offer a means for measuring various targets, such as increasing the revenue from 5 to 7 percent, the achievement of these goals is contingent upon budget allocations and meeting revenue goals to fund future objectives. Thus, it is first necessary to determine the plan's priorities and the costs associated with their execution. Then comes the balancing act—weighing what needs to be accomplished with what is affordable.

In a strategic context, numerous scenarios or options may be selected, and each can be interlinked with existing and new marketing strategies. For example, "If we exceed our revenue growth goal of 5 percent in year one, we will move to Option Two, increase the budget, and accelerate the infrastructure development." Let's now take a look at a theoretical budget and planning concept for the strategic tourism marketing plan for Your City.

BUDGET AND PLANNING SUMMARY

With the current hotel occupancy tax at 5 percent, Your City generates approximately $450,000 annually to its tourism fund. At the 5 percent city level, Your City is almost 2 percent less than the adjacent metropolitan city in its hotel tax, which is at 7 percent. There is no perceivable difference between the areas in the eyes of the guests—Your City's lodging facility's actual addresses are in the same metropolitan area. It is recommended that consideration be given to increasing the tax from 5 percent to 7 percent to equal that of the metropolis. This will generate an incremental $180,000 annually to Your City's tourism fund, or almost $1.2 million over a five-year period. Tables 4 and 5 outline the base fund levels at 5 percent, 6 percent, and 7 percent, respectively, for the next five years. Additionally, three growth levels are calculated at plus 5 percent, plus 7 percent, and plus 9 percent on an annualized basis for the five-year period. Note the difference between the 5 percent base level and the 7 percent base level over the entire period of the plan.

Another consideration during the budget planning process is the use of the zero-based budget approach. This approach basically begins the process with a zero dollar balance and then adds the actual amounts for the most important items in the execution of the plan. *The most important items are defined as those items or activities that directly contribute to room nights, increase overnight visitors, and add to the hotel rate, such as promotions and group sales.* In addition, this approach is based on actual measurement; if a promotion costs $1,000 to launch or a staff person costs $20,000 in expense, the expectation is a five times return or $5,000 for the launch and $100,000 in productivity. The items with the highest returns are the priorities.

TABLE 4. Base Funding Levels—Year One to Year Five

	Annualized Growth Rates	Year One	Year Two	Year Three	Year Four	Year Five
Current Base Level $450,000 at 5% tax rate	5%	$472,500	$496,125	$520,931	$546,978	$574,327
	7%	$481,000	$515,205	$551,269	$589,857	$631,147
	9%	$490,500	$534,645	$582,763	$635,212	$692,381
Current Base Level $540,000 at 6% tax rate	5%	$567,000	$595,350	$625,118	$656,374	$689,193
	7%	$577,800	$618,246	$661,523	$707,830	$750,300
	9%	$588,560	$641,574	$699,315	$762,253	$830,856
Current Base Level $630,000 at 7% tax rate	5%	$661,500	$694,575	$729,304	$765,769	$804,057
	7%	$674,100	$721,287	$771,777	$825,801	$883,607
	9%	$686,700	$748,503	$815,868	$889,296	$969,333

Note: The cumulative variance in marketing funds between a 5 percent rate and a 7 percent rate over the five-year period amounts to $1,222,344 (assuming a 5 percent growth rate).

TABLE 5. Incremental Tourism Marketing Dollars
at 7 Percent versus 5 Percent Rate—Year One to Year Five*

Year	Variance
Base Year	+$180,000
Year One	+$189,000
Year Two	+$198,540
Year Three	+$208,373
Year Four	+$218,791
Year Five	+$229,730
Cumulative Total	+$1,224,344

* Assumes a 5 percent growth rate

Here are a number of key points to focus on during the prioritization process:

- Effective promotions produce strong room nights numbers and improve market share.
- Public relations can be a relatively low-cost, high-return weapon.
- Cooperatives stretch marketing dollars as well as improve their reach.
- Direct sales comes with a high expense and therefore must produce high returns.
- Revenue is generated by a combination of promotions, advertising, and sales, whereas image is produced by public relations.

Given these focal points and taking into consideration Your City's tourism marketing needs as outlined in this plan, several budget allocation options are proposed for the base year as well as in general for the next five years.

Option One

This option utilizes promotions, related support advertising, and co-ops as the main focuses of the plan. Public relations and the need for a full-time agency or tourism marketing function are also recognized.

TABLE 6. Year One Recommended Budget Allocations (Option One)

	Amount ($)	Percentage of Base*
Promotions	50,000	11.1
Advertising**	185,000	41.1
Co-Op Funds***	50,000	11.1
Public Relations/Communications	30,000	6.7
Sales/Special Events	35,000	7.8
Salaries/Fees and All Related Expenses	50,000	7.8
C&VB Support	50,000	11.1
Misc./Transfer to General Fund	N/A	N/A
TOTAL	450,000	100.0

* Assumes a $450,000 base
** In support of promotions
*** Incremental advertising and promotions usage

Option Two

This option is based on the premise that the visual perception of Your City is a marketing problem that needs quick resolution. It suggests that in the base year, the budget for tourism marketing remain "spread" as was outlined in Option 1, followed by an increased room occupancy tax of 2 percent through the use of a visual perceptions co-op. The purpose of this co-op in Year One is to seek matching funds from the metropolitan attraction, the state, and other agencies to address the key issues of the visual entry points to the city and other marketing-oriented infrastructure items, including signs at the attraction and international tourism signs related to international food and beverage facilities.

TABLE 7. Year One Recommended Budget Allocations (Option Two)

	Amount ($)	Percentage of Base*
Promotions	50,000	11.1
Advertising**	185,000	41.1
Co-Op Funds***	50,000	11.1
Public Relations/Communications	30,000	6.7
Sales/Special Events	35,000	7.8
Salaries/Fees and All Related Expenses	50,000	7.8
C&VB Support	50,000	11.1
Misc./Transfer to General Fund	N/A	N/A
SUBTOTAL	450,000	100.0
Visual Perceptions Improvements	180,000	100 of new funds
TOTAL	630,000	100.0

* Assumes a $450,000 base
** In support of promotions
*** Incremental advertising and promotions usage

Option Three

This option assumes the incremental funding level from the additional 2 percent in revenue, based on a total budget of $630,000. Excluded are any allocations to visual perceptions improvements. All revenue dollars are channeled to tourism marketing weaponry. This particular budget is recommended to maximize revenue growth, provided the problems of visual perceptions can be suitably addressed with alternative funds.

TABLE 8. Year One Recommended Budget Allocations (Option Three)

	Amount ($)	Percentage of Base*
Promotions	60,000	9.5
Advertising**	245,000	38.8
Co-Op Funds***	100,000	15.9
Public Relations/Communications****	50,000	7.9
Sales	45,000	7.1
Salaries/Fees and All Related Expenses	60,000	9.5
C&VB Support	70,000	11.1
Misc./Transfer to General Fund	N/A	N/A
TOTAL	630,000	100.0*

* Adds to 100 percent due to rounding
** In support of promotions and includes agency commissions
*** Incremental advertising and promotional support
**** Includes agency fee for public relations/communication services

Option Four

This option maintains the status quo and is not recommended for the overall planning period nor is it favored for Year One of the plan. It is presented here to enable the allocation of new funds (i.e., 2 percent) to increase the room night revenue-producing areas of the budget while maintaining all other areas at the base budget of $450,000.

TABLE 9. Year One Status Quo Budget Allocations Including Additional Funds (Option Four)

	Amount ($)	Percentage of Base*
Base Funding		
Promotions	0	0
Advertising	146,250	32.5
Co-Op Funds	0	0
Public Relations/Communications	0	0
Sales/Special Events	25,650	5.7
Salaries/Fees and All Related Expenses***	59,850	13.3
C&VB Support**	90,000	20.0
Misc./Transfer to General Fund****	97,650	21.7
Unallocated	30,600	6.8
SUBTOTAL	450,000	100.0
New Funding		Percentage of New Funding
Add to Special Events	9,150*****	5.1
Add to Advertising	53,750*****	29.9
Add to Co-Op	41,250	22.9
Add to PR/Communications	25,000	13.9
SUBTOTAL	129,150	
GRAND TOTAL	579,150	

* Base budget of $450,000
** $90,000 current support level
*** Includes: office supplies, salaries, social security, auto allowance, insurance, utilities, training, dues and fees, equipment rental, contract services
**** Miscellaneous includes: capital outlays, transfer to general fund
***** Restores to previous year's fiscal year levels

In all of the previous budgets (excluding Option Four), an attempt has been made to allocate tourism marketing dollars to areas with a direct effect on increased room night revenue. The need to improve the visual perception of Your City is essential to both visitor retention and to increased room rates and revenues.

Beyond Year One, the same proportionate allocations should be maintained with incremental dollars being channeled to room night–producing events and additional support for public relations. However, this recommendation assumes that infrastructure-related concerns are addressed.

THE APPENDIX

The final section of a strategic tourism marketing plan is the appendix. Although appendixes are often included within the original document, it is suggested here that relevant statistical data and research findings are presented in an accompanying volume. This will ensure that the marketing plan remains an action document and is not weighted down with excessive numbers and data. A sample of items that form an appendix are as follows:

APPENDIX

I. Tourism Fund Review Chart

II. Research Findings from Metropolitan Area Attraction

III. Distribution of State and City Tourism Dollars

IV. Metropolitan City Area Calendar of Events

V. Metropolitan City Area Current Meeting Planners Guide

VI. Contacts List for Research Information and Potential Co-Op Partners

CONCLUSION

A strategic tourism marketing plan offers many benefits for cities, towns, and tourist destinations. However, the most significant benefit is the enhanced revenues for your community. Since we have outlined in detail how to prepare such a plan using Your City, U.S.A., we have also included several work forms in the next section to help you with key components of your plan. These forms will assist you in both the development and implementation of your city's strategic tourism marketing plan.

PART TWO:
WORK FORMS

Form A. Target Markets

IN-STATE, TOP FIVE FEEDER MARKETS   % of Visitors

Leisure: 1. _____ Est. %

2. _____

3. _____

4. _____

5. _____

Business: 1. _____ Est. %

2. _____

3. _____

4. _____

5. _____

OTHER STATES, TOP FIVE FEEDER MARKETS

Leisure: 1. _____ Est. %

2. _____

3. _____

4. _____

5. _____

Business: 1. _____ Est. %

2. _____

3. _____

4. _____

5. _____

INTERNATIONAL, TOP FIVE FEEDER MARKETS

Leisure: 1. _____ Est. %

2. _____

3. _____

4. _____

5. _____

Business: 1. _____ Est. %

2. _____

3. _____

4. _____

5. _____

Form B. Visual Perceptions*

IDENTIFY THE TOP FIVE POSITIVE VISUAL PERCEPTIONS OF YOUR CITY.

1. _____

2. _____

3. _____

4. _____

5. _____

IDENTIFY THE FIVE MOST NEGATIVE VISUAL PERCEPTIONS OF YOUR CITY.

1. _____

2. _____

3. _____

4. _____

5. _____

*Use a leisure and business traveler's perspective, beginning with his or her point of entry to your city and proceeding to key attraction areas.

Form C: Competitive Assessment*

LIST YOUR TOP FIVE STRENGTHS AS A DESTINATION.

Leisure: 1. _____

2. _____

3. _____

4. _____

5. _____

Business: 1. _____

2. _____

3. _____

4. _____

5. _____

LIST THE TOP FIVE WEAKNESSES OF YOUR CITY.

Leisure: 1. _____

2. _____

3. _____

4. _____

5. _____

Business: 1. _____

2. _____

3. _____

4. _____

5. _____

*Use the leisure and business traveler's perspective, not your own.

Form D. Opportunities

LIST FIVE OPPORTUNITIES TO IMPROVE OR CREATE NEW ATTRACTIONS OR INFRASTRUCTURE.

1. _____

2. _____

3. _____

4. _____

5. _____

IDENTIFY FIVE CO-OP PARTNERS OR TARGETS TO ENHANCE THE MARKETING AND DEVELOPMENT OF YOUR CITY.

1. _____

2. _____

3. _____

4. _____

5. _____

Form E. Mission

MISSION STATEMENT:

SLOGAN OR OTHER IDENTIFIER:

Form F. Objectives

QUALIFIED:

1. Increase visitor count by _____

2. Increase revenues by _____

3. Etc. _____

4. Etc. _____

5. Etc. _____

QUALITATIVE:

1. Improve _____

2. Enhance _____

3. Etc. _____

4. Etc. _____

5. Etc. _____

Form G. Promotions Plan

FISCAL YEAR	1st 90 Days	2nd 90 Days	3rd 90 Days	4th 90 Days
Promo #1				
Promo #2				
Promo #3				
Promo #4				
Promo #5				
Promo #6				
Promo #7				
Promo #8				

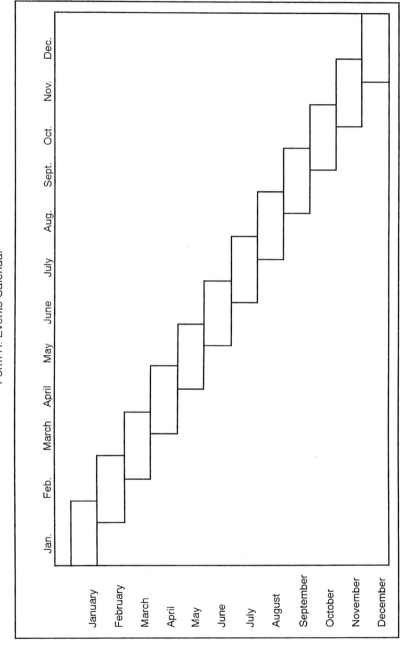

Form H. Events Calendar

Form I. Prioritization

LIST THE TOP FIVE PRIORITIES FOR:*

Generating Increased Visitation

Leisure travelers: 1. _____

2. _____

3. _____

4. _____

5. _____

Business travelers: 1. _____

2. _____

3. _____

4. _____

5. _____

Improving the Visual Perception for Your Visitors

1. _____

2. _____

3. _____

4. _____

5. _____

*These may come from the promotions plans or events calendars or other marketing strategies.

Form J. Revenue and Reallocation

IDENTIFY NEW OR INCREMENTAL SOURCES OF REVENUE.

New:

1. _____
2. _____
3. _____
4. _____
5. _____

Incremental:

1. _____
2. _____
3. _____
4. _____
5. _____

IDENTIFY WHERE RESOURCES NEED TO BE REALLOCATED
TO ACHIEVE PLAN GOALS/OBJECTIVES.

From:

1. _____
2. _____
3. _____
4. _____
5. _____

To:

1. _____
2. _____
3. _____
4. _____
5. _____

Form K. Marketing Budget

	DOLLARS	PERCENT OF TOTAL
ADVERTISING		
PROMOTIONS		
PUBLIC RELATIONS		
SALES		
SPECIAL EVENTS		
CVB SUPPORT		
VISUAL PERCEPTION IMPROVEMENTS		
CO-OP FUNDS		
OTHER TRANSFERS TO THE BUDGET/FUND		
TOTAL		

Notes

1. Chon, Kye-Sung and Olsen, Michael D. (1990). Applying the strategic management process in the management of tourism organizations. *Tourism Management*, 11(3), p. 207.

2. Hiebing, Roman B., Jr. and Cooper, Scott W. (1997). *The Successful Marketing Plan: A Disciplined and Comprehensive Approach*, Second edition. Lincolnwood, IL: NTC Business Books.

3. Chon, Kye-Sung and Olsen, Michael D. (1990). Applying the strategic management process in the management of tourism organizations. *Tourism Management*, 11(3), p. 207.

4. Hiebing, Roman G., Jr. and Cooper, Scott W. (1997). *The Successful Marketing Plan: A Disciplined and Comprehensive Approach*, Second edition. Lincolnwood, IL: NTC Business Books.

5. Kotler, Philip (Ed.) (1986). *Principles of Marketing*. Englewood Cliffs, NJ: Prentice-Hall.

6. Hiebing, Roman G., Jr. and Cooper, Scott W. (1997). *The Successful Marketing Plan: A Disciplined and Comprehensive Approach*, Second edition. Lincolnwood, IL: NTC Business Books.

7. Hiebing, Roman G., Jr. and Cooper, Scott W. (1997). *The Successful Marketing Plan: A Disciplined and Comprehensive Approach*, Second edition, Lincolnwood, IL: NTC Business Books.

8. Chon, Kye-Sung. (1995). *Welcome to Hospitality*. Albany, NY: Delmar Publishers, p. 129.

9. Nykiel, Ronald A. (1997). *Marketing in the Hospitality Industry*, Third edition. East Lansing, MI: Educational Institute of the American Hotel and Motel Association.

10. Hiebing, Roman G., Jr. and Cooper, Scott W. (1997). *The Successful Marketing Plan: A Disciplined and Comprehensive Approach*, Second edition. Lincolnwood, IL: NTC Business Books.

11. Hiebing, Roman G., Jr. and Cooper, Scott W. (1997). *The Successful Marketing Plan: A Disciplined and Comprehensive Approach*, Second edition. Lincolnwood, IL: NTC Business Books.

12. Nykiel, Ronald A. (1997). *Marketing in the Hospitality Industry*, Third edition. East Lansing, MI: Educational Institute of the American Hotel and Motel Association.

13. Chon, Kye-Sung and Olsen, Michael D. (1990). Applying the strategic management process in the management of tourism organizations. *Tourism Management*, 11(3), p. 213.

Bibliography

Chon, Kye-Sung and Olsen, Michael D. (1990). Applying the strategic management process in the management of tourism organizations. *Tourism Management*, 11(3), p. 207.

Chon, Kye-Sung. (1995). *Welcome To Hospitality.* Albany, NY: Delmar Publishers.

Coltman, Michael M. (1989). *Tourism Marketing.* New York: Van Nostrand Reinhold.

Cravens, David W. (1987). *Strategic Marketing,* Second edition. Homewood, IL: Richard D. Irwin.

Crompton, John L. and Lamb, C. W. (1986). *Marketing Government and Social Services.* New York: John Wiley and Sons.

Haywood, Michael K. (1986). "Can the tourist area life cycle be made operational?" *Tourism Management,* 7(3), pp. 154-167.

Heath, Ernie and Wall, Geoffrey (1992). *Marketing Tourism Destinations: A Strategic Planning Approach.* New York: John Wiley and Sons.

Hiebing, Roman G., Jr. and Cooper, Scott W. (1997). *Successful Marketing Plan: A Disciplined and Comprehensive Approach,* Second edition. Lincolnwood, IL: NTC Business Books.

Kaynak, Erdener. (1985). Developing marketing strategy for a resource-based industry. *Tourism Management,* 6(3), pp. 184-193.

Kotler, Philip (Ed.) (1986). *Principles of Marketing.* Englewood Cliffs, NJ: Prentice-Hall.

McIntosh, Robert W. and Goeldner, Charles R. (1990). *Tourism: Principles, Practices and Philosophies,* Sixth edition. New York: John Wiley and Sons.

Mill, Robert C. and Morrison, Alastair M. (1985). *The Tourism System: An Introductory Text.* Englewood Cliffs, NJ: Prentice-Hall.

Murphy, Peter E. (1983). Tourism as a community industry. *Tourism Management,* 4(3), pp. 180-193.

Nykiel, Ronald A. (1997) *Marketing in the Hospitality Industry,* third edition. Educational Institute of the American Hotel and Motel Association, East Lansing, MI.

Reime, Mathias and Hawkins, Cameron (1985). Planning and developing hospitality facilities that increase tourism demand. In Hawkins, Donald E. Shafer, and E. L. Rovelstadt (Eds.), *Tourism Marketing and Marketing Issues.* Washington, DC: Washington University Press, pp. 337-355.

Smith, Stephen L. R. (1988). Defining tourism: A supply-side view. *Annals of Tourism Research,* 15(2), pp. 179-190.

Wahab, Salah, Crampon, L. J., and Rothfield, L. M. (1976). *Tourism Marketing.* London: Tourism International Press.

Index

Page numbers followed by the letter "t" indicate tables; those followed by the letter "f" indicate figures.

Order Your Own Copy of
This Important Book for Your Personal Library!

MARKETING YOUR CITY, U.S.A.
A Guide to Developing a Strategic Tourism Marketing Plan

_____ in hardbound at $29.95 (ISBN: 0-7890-0591-3)

_____ in softbound at $19.95 (ISBN: 0-7890-0592-1)

COST OF BOOKS _____

OUTSIDE USA/CANADA/
MEXICO: ADD 20% _____

POSTAGE & HANDLING _____
(US: $3.00 for first book & $1.25
for each additional book)
Outside US: $4.75 for first book
& $1.75 for each additional book)

SUBTOTAL _____

IN CANADA: ADD 7% GST _____

STATE TAX _____
(NY, OH & MN residents, please
add appropriate local sales tax)

FINAL TOTAL _____
(If paying in Canadian funds,
convert using the current
exchange rate. UNESCO
coupons welcome.)

☐ **BILL ME LATER:** ($5 service charge will be added)
(Bill-me option is good on US/Canada/Mexico orders only;
not good to jobbers, wholesalers, or subscription agencies.)

☐ Check here if billing address is different from
shipping address and attach purchase order and
billing address information.

Signature _____

☐ **PAYMENT ENCLOSED: $** _____

☐ **PLEASE CHARGE TO MY CREDIT CARD.**

☐ Visa   ☐ MasterCard   ☐ AmEx   ☐ Discover
☐ Diner's Club

Account # _____

Exp. Date _____

Signature _____

Prices in US dollars and subject to change without notice.

NAME _____

INSTITUTION _____

ADDRESS _____

CITY _____

STATE/ZIP _____

COUNTRY _____ COUNTY (NY residents only) _____

TEL _____ FAX _____

E-MAIL _____
May we use your e-mail address for confirmations and other types of information? ☐ Yes   ☐ No

Order From Your Local Bookstore or Directly From
The Haworth Press, Inc.
10 Alice Street, Binghamton, New York 13904-1580 • USA
TELEPHONE: 1-800-HAWORTH (1-800-429-6784) / Outside US/Canada: (607) 722-5857
FAX: 1-800-895-0582 / Outside US/Canada: (607) 772-6362
E-mail: getinfo@haworthpressinc.com
PLEASE PHOTOCOPY THIS FORM FOR YOUR PERSONAL USE.

BOF96

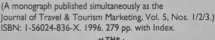